Lowcountry Herald:

Helping the Homeless in the Holy City

L. Shay Rockhold

DEDICATION

This book is dedicated to every person who sees a fellow human being in need, feels compassion, and works to change the world and make it a better place.

CONTENTS

ACKNOWLEDGMENTS

Thank you to everyone who let me interview them for this project.

May your dedication be greatly rewarded.

1
HOW MUCH OF A PROBLEM IS HOMELESSNESS?

No one denies that homelessness is a problem in the US. It's evident in the news on TV, and it's also evident by what we see as we travel throughout our day.

But how much of a problem is it? Do our eyes deceive us, or perhaps the media are blowing things out of proportion?

Let's take a look at some statistics:

- The number of people that are homeless for some period in a given year is estimated at over 3 million people.
- This represents as much as 1 percent of our population.
- The number of long-term homeless is around 1,750,000.
- The average monthly income for a homeless individual is approximately $350.
- 28% don't get enough to eat daily.
- 40% are veterans.
- 66% have some issue with drug abuse, alcohol abuse, or mental illness.
- 44% do some sort of paid work, (even if it is sporadic).
- 25% have steady employment.

- 46% cite domestic abuse as a reason for homelessness.
- 36% of the homeless are families with children.

Becoming homeless can happen to anyone. Being laid off for a month with no savings to live on can be enough to trigger a domino effect and create a homeless situation down the road.

With so many Americans living paycheck to paycheck, homelessness is a looming threat for the majority of households.

If you couple this financial reality with the fact that many people don't have extended family with which they can reside while they "get back on their feet,' you have an even bigger problem.

What about South Carolina?

In South Carolina, there are over 6000 homeless, and about 400 of those reside in Charleston County. Across the state, there are approximately 11 homeless out of every 10,000 residents.

Compared to Georgia, we're about half of their rate. We're slightly lower than North Carolina and Tennessee.

However, our numbers are nothing to celebrate. Even one person going with out shelter is one too many.

2
WHAT IS A STREET NEWSPAPER?

Unless an individual who is homeless has a job when they lose their housing, they are faced with a disheartening Catch-22: they can't find a job without a permanent address, and they can't get a permanent address without a job.

Since getting hired for a traditional job under such circumstances is such a challenge, the idea for a newspaper (or magazine) that was written about the homeless (and often with article contributions from the homeless) in order to be sold by the homeless was born. Articles may also cover issues such as poverty and other challenges faced by the homeless.

The beginning of this movement began in 1986 in Oregon, and a similar type of paper was started in New York in 1989. The New York paper is still in production.

The basic idea is this:

- A newspaper or magazine is created.
- The vendors are homeless individuals.
- The initial supply of papers is given for free.
- After that initial supply, the vendor must then pay for future papers.
- The vendors keep the profits from all sales.

A typical example is the New York publication:

vendors pay $0.50 per copy, and the asking price is $1.25 per copy. The vendors keep any profits. (Some people buying the papers pay more than the listed price as an additional benefit for the vendor.)

In addition to the money for vendors purchasing copies, most street papers also sell advertising and accept donations.

3

WHAT HAS BEEN DONE ELSEWHERE?

According to the International Network of Street Newspapers, there are over 120 street newspapers published in 41 countries. These papers serve 14,000 homeless vendors, and have a readership of 6,000,000 people. (There are also independent papers that are not members of the INSP, and those papers bring these totals even higher.)

In the United States, there are over 30 street newspapers published in various cities.

Here are some stats from various papers that have been in operation for a while:

- *The Big Issue* in London sells 122,000 copies of their publication each week through 550 vendors. 60% of their revenue comes from publication sales.
- *Real Change* in Seattle sells 20,000 copies every two weeks.
- *The Contributor* in Seattle has a circulation of 120,000 copies per month. Papers are purchased for $0.75 and are sold for $2 each. They have around 400 active vendors. 35 percent of their vendors have found housing since becoming vendors for the paper. They also have ways for vendors to earn merchandise, clothing, and more through meeting quotas and sales goals.

- *One Step Away* in Philadelphia, PA, has an impressive track record. The majority of their vendors have been able to secure permanent housing with their income from *One Step Away*. For 79% of their vendors, *One Step Away* is their sole source of income.
- *Toledo Streets* in Toledo, OH, has over 160 vendors and has sold over 16,000 copies of their publication.

Looking at the revenue for papers in other cities is interesting and inspiring, as well:

- On average, less than half of revenues were generated by magazine sales.
- Ad sales comprised 15-30% of total revenues.
- Charitable donations often made up 10-30% of revenues.
- Some papers also incorporated merchandise sales for a small part (less than 10%) of their revenue.
- Additional income streams made it easier for street papers to get started and to operate through high and low cycles.

4

THE VISION FOR CHARLESTON

Seeing what has been done in other areas inspires a great deal of hope in those who seek to help the homeless of Charleston and the surrounding areas.

The *Lowcountry Herald* is the monthly street magazine in Charleston, SC. The mission of the Lowcountry Herald is as follows:

> *"The mission of the* Lowcountry Herald *is to produce a quality print publication to be sold to homeless people and people living in poverty in Charleston, SC, who may resell the publication and generate an income to lift themselves out of poverty and live a life of dignity"*

The philosophy of the magazine is a noble one:

> *"Street paper vendors purchase copies of their local street paper at a portion of the cover price and become micro entrepreneurs, selling their product on the streets, to earn their own living and support themselves and their families. This has the advantage of giving them a way to make cash that doesn't depend on their mental state, background, education, criminal record, employment history, housing status or any of the other factors that keep the homeless from working."*

Paul Gangarosa, the owner and President of the Board for the *Lowcountry Herald*, started with the idea of a street paper that would empower the homeless, letting them work to improve their situation, regardless of their background or difficulties.

He shared this vision with others and gathered a team to help make this vision a reality:

- Sharon McAllister – Vice President of the Board
- Jill Hunter Powell – Managing Editor
- Ryan Smiley - Editor
- Rachel Duley - Vendor Coordinator

This is a project that was five years in the making, and everyone has come on board because they truly want to make a difference for the homeless in the Holy City.

Speaking with everyone it is quite clear how passionate they are about this cause. It's evident in everything they say about it, and they all want to see this publication grow.

"I would like to see the *Lowcountry Herald* explode in the next year with 50 or 100 vendors all across town." This is the sentiment expressed by Jill, and the others involved share similar hopes.

"I'd been homeless previously, so this really touched me," Rachel said when I spoke with her. "I was homeless for a year with my mom, and we had nothing available like [this] to help us. I thought it would be a really good opportunity for others."

"I would love to see the *Lowcountry Herald* being distributed all around Charleston and having the community become involved in our cause," shared Ryan. "I really love the idea of helping people help themselves.," she added.

When asked about future goals, Paul quickly said that "more vendors" topped the list. "I'd like to see us grow at the rate of about 10 vendors a month, [...] and actually selling enough [copies] every month so that they want to keep coming back and sell more."

With the success of street newspapers in other cities, it's clear that the potential to help the homeless of Charleston and the surrounding areas is within reach.

The Lowcountry Herald provides a simple, tangible way to help the homeless help themselves. There has been so much success in helping street paper vendors transition into stable, permanent housing in areas with community support and a solid network of vendors, advocates, and volunteers.

10

5
HOW YOU CAN HELP

The Lowcountry Herald has a number of ways you can get involved in this worthwhile cause.

First and foremost would be to buy the paper. There are also a number of other ways to help:

- **Spread the word among those who work with the homeless or with those you may know who are facing this challenge. More vendors are needed to sell the paper.**
- Support local vendors that you see selling the Lowcountry Herald. Get to know them. Make a point of stopping by and buying a copy on a regular basis.
- **Advertising can be a substantial part of a street newspaper's revenue. Consider purchasing advertising for your business or organization.**
- Donations are also a way of supporting this cause. One-time and monthly donations are welcome.
- **Share the good news about what Lowcountry Herald is doing. Talk to business leaders, churches, ministries, and any other groups that might be able to help through purchasing advertising or through monthly financial support.**
- Do you have a location where vendors can sell their copies of the paper? Locations are needed.

- **Like the Facebook page and share it with everyone you know.**
- Purchase a copy of the magazine and tell your friends to be looking for vendors.
- **Share your copy! Let your friends and family know how enjoyable the publication is.**
- Show your support for the advertisers. Be sure to let them know you saw the ad in the *Lowcountry Herald* when you respond to the ads.
- **Help make it simple for the vendors to do business within the city. If you hear of "red tape" making it harder for vendors to do business, get involved however you can to make the process easier.**

FOR MORE INFORMATION

- Please visit them on the web at www.LowcountryHerald.org.

- Like them on Facebook: https://www.Facebook.com/lowcountryherald

- Call them at (843) 442-1486

- Email them at LowcountryHerald@gmail.com

SOURCES

- National Law Center on Homelessness and Poverty

- *Post and Courier*, June 26, 2013

- International Network of Street Newspapers

- *Lowcountry Herald*

ABOUT THE AUTHOR

L. Shay Rockhold is a mom of 3, writer, published author, sci-fi fan, coffee addict, public speaker, business owner and Candy Land champion.

She is the Organizer of the Carolina Business Outreach Network, a group of over 400 business professionals in the Charleston, SC, area.

Shay enjoys learning about how people are trying to change the world and make it a better place. Sharing stories that are positive, uplifting, and motivational is what makes her business a daily dose of awesome.

ABOUT ROCKHOLD PUBLISHING

Rockhold Publishing believes that every person has a remarkable story to share.

We work with individuals and groups in order to help share stories of all kinds.

With non-profit groups, we gather the stories of those involved in order to create a unique, professionally-published book. That book can then be used as a fundraiser. We call this "Purpose-fueled Fundraising," and it's very different from traditional fundraising.

For students and schools, we can help the students get published. We can work with individual students, whole classrooms, or the entire school. The students get published, and the books can be used to raise funds for the school.

For individuals, we share stories of success, triumph, personal testimonies, business, and so much more.

For more information, please visit our website:

www.RockholdPublishing.com